Michael Worker
Cleveland, QLD
2/07

ATTRACTING Butterflies to your Garden

Published in Australia by
Reed New Holland
an imprint of New Holland Publishers (Australia) Pty Ltd
Sydney • Auckland • London • Cape Town
14 Aquatic Drive Frenchs Forest NSW 2086 Australia
218 Lake Road Northcote Auckland New Zealand
24 Nutford Place London W1H 6DQ United Kingdom
80 McKenzie Street Cape Town 8001 South Africa

First published in 1990 by Reed Books.
Reprinted in 1996.
This edition published in 2000 by Reed New Holland.

National Library of Australia Cataloguing-in-Publication Data:

Clyne, Densey, 1926–.
Attracting butterflies to your garden.

ISBN 1 876334 56 8.

1. Butterflies—Australia. 2. Butterfly attracting. I. Title.

595.7890994

Publishing Manager: Louise Egerton
Cover design: Peta Zoubakin
Illustrations: Helen McCosker
Printer: South China Printing Company Ltd, Hong Kong

ATTRACTING
Butterflies
to your Garden

Densey Clyne

Contents

Introduction

Making butterflies welcome

Everybody loves butterflies. Ants may aggravate you, beetles may bore you and termites will certainly put you in a turmoil! But a butterfly is the one insect universally approved as it floats on the warm summer air, flies and flirts among the flowers, sips ambrosia in the sunshine and does no harm to anyone.

Trouble is, we see a butterfly flitting across the garden, or stopping briefly at a flower and we say, 'Oh, look, isn't it pretty?' or write a poem, or simply take it for granted. Which does nothing at all to make a butterfly feel welcome or inspire it to set up house and raise a family. It comes briefly from nowhere, touches down on a flower or two then vanishes over the garden fence. And that's that!

Yes, but that needn't be that. We can encourage butterflies to be a permanent part of the garden scene. Our flowers won't mind. After all, flowers and butterflies were in partnership millions of years before we came on the scene. As for our human fears and phobias – well, butterflies have the advantage of being stingless, non-aggressive and very visible. You know where you are with butterflies. And how could they help liking us in return for the free meals we give them?

Any garden plot can attract butterflies, but you'll undoubtedly see more of them in an overgrown garden that romps and riots, a garden that's a little wild, where self-sown seeds mix happily with small inoffensive weeds and wildings, and just once in a while lawn lapses into meadow. In fact, it's the lazy gardener who's most likely to produce the best annual crop of 'flying flowers'. But without going overboard there are practical ways of turning any garden, large or small, formal or informal, country or suburban, into a butterfly garden.

Two mouths to feed

The important thing to remember is that a butterfly leads a double life. Before it takes to the air as a winged beauty with mating and reproduction in mind, it must survive many months as a sexless caterpillar with a one-track mouth. So if we want lots of butterflies, we must think about the requirements of caterpillars. Our garden can supply these without being reduced to a wasteland.

You may think that caterpillars and gardens simply don't go together. When it comes to caterpillars most gardeners are ruthless in defence of their helpless charges, and rightly so. But with the obvious exception of the introduced cabbage white butterfly, it's the caterpillars of moths rather than butterflies that do the real damage. No native Australian butterflies are known to be unduly harmful to garden plants. In fact, a butterfly caterpillar wouldn't know what to do with a rose, dahlia or daffodil if it was offered on a golden stem.

So bear in mind that the caterpillar you're thinking of squashing may not be a despoiler of your garden treasures at all but a butterfly-in-waiting. It all depends what it's feeding on. If you want a butterfly bonanza it's important that you are able to relate a caterpillar (1) to the butterfly it will become, and (2) to the plants you'll find it on.

Food for caterpillars

A butterfly doesn't grow. A small butterfly is small because that's the proper size for its kind. It's the caterpillar that grows, and bodybuilding is its only interest in life. Forget about fun among the foliage – before a caterpillar's mind can turn even remotely to thoughts of love its body weight must be increased several thousandfold. A caterpillar is a living machine designed to turn green stuff into caterpillar stuff. Its life is one long meal with short breaks for digestion.

But caterpillar meals are gourmet meals. And if a caterpillar has a taste for Milkweed Ragout you'll never tempt it with Camphor Laurel Bonne Femme. A butterfly bears this well in mind when she chooses a leaf to lay her eggs on. Over millions of years the caterpillars or larvae of Australian butterflies have evolved alongside our native plants. Some are adapted to only one kind of plant, others to a group of closely related plants. At the far end of the scale are a few with a wide range of native foodplants, not necessarily related to each other.

Since European settlement a few native butterflies have adopted our introduced ornamentals, crops or weeds as larval foodplants. Some of these 'exotics' have come to be preferred over the traditional native plants. The cultivated plants have the advantage of lush growth under ideal conditions of soil, water and loving care. A well-known example is the introduced camphor laurel, a street and garden tree that has become truly Australian. It has certainly been given the seal of approval by some of our most attractive butterflies. Other butterflies have adapted to commercial citrus trees. In all cases the exotic foodplants are related to the butterflies' traditional native foodplants.

It may not be every gardener's joy to give room to weeds and wayside vagrants, but some of the less invasive ones are worth a place for the butterflies that have adopted them. Such butterfly attractants as purple top, white clover, milkweed and Scotch thistle can even be seen as attractive in their own right. And it's surely better to recycle them as butterfly food than to poison or burn them.

If you are one of those who draw the line at providing board and lodging for any kind of caterpillar, no matter how discreetly it feeds, then never mind. You can simply set out to lure more butterflies over the garden fence by growing suitable flowers.

Food for butterflies

It's a pleasant thought that in learning about butterflies we can also learn a little more about the flowers in our gardens. Flowers are pretty not on our account but in order to advertise and sell a commodity. Those intricate designs and brilliant colours are there for a purpose. They are the 'commercials' of the plant world.

Butterflies need plenty of carbohydrate to fuel their flight muscles. Flowering plants provide this in the form of sweet nectar, and the exquisite containers it comes in are specifically designed to catch the colour-sensitive eyes of their pollinators. As everyone knows, nectar is the reward for the transfer of pollen from flower to flower, and butterflies do this very well.

Many plants aim their advertising specifically or mainly at the butterfly market, using shapes, forms and colours that will attract butterflies to buy. Such plants are referred to as psychophilous, meaning 'butterfly-loving', and they take into account certain characteristics that butterflies have.

1. *Butterflies are creatures of the light, so the flowers produce their nectar during the day.*
2. *Butterflies share excellent colour vision with birds and people. They can even see some colours invisible to us, such as infra-red. It's been found that some kinds of butterfly prefer certain colours over others - swallowtails prefer red - but the important thing is that flower colours should be bright.*
3. *Unlike moths, butterflies don't rely much on scent to guide them to nectar. Flowers pollinated by butterflies rarely have more than a faint, though pleasant, perfume.*
4. *To guide the butterfly's long, delicate 'tongue' or sucking tube quickly to the nectar, typical butterfly flowers have their nectaries deep inside a narrow, smooth-walled tube or spur, or at the base of a groove or channel. While the butterfly probes, it picks up pollen on its head or elsewhere. The narrow tube also serves to keep less desirable insects from stealing the nectar.*
5. *Butterflies prefer flowers they can stay on for a while without wasting too much energy in flight. For this, butterfly flowers provide plenty of nectar and some kind of platform for their visitors to stand on. The platform may be a single broad petal, a flat rim of petals around a single nectar container, or a flower spike or head with many single flowers close together. The following are some garden flowers I would personally recommend for butterflies.*

Buddleia *deserves the common name of 'butterfly bush' by which its known in many parts of the world. (Some other butterfly bushes are so named for the shape of their flowers.) A platform for the butterfly's dainty feet is provided by the densely crowded, tubular flowers that form the showy flower spikes. A purple or lilac buddleia bush in full bloom is seldom without butterfly visitors, whether it's in a tropical garden or a temperate one. Similar in shape to buddleia, cool-country lilacs offer the same advantages.*

Lantana *is a South American shrub that has become a pest species here, but butterfly lovers have to admit it has one saving grace—wherever it grows along roadsides and bush clearings it attracts our native butterflies like no other wild plant. The harmless garden forms or cultivars of lantana come in many colours and stay properly in their place. They form domed flowerheads with pretty, tubular florets opening in succession at the centre.*

Veronica, verbena, valerian *and* ***phlox*** *are among the plants with closely packed flowers in the right colours for butterflies.*

Milkweed*. In my garden I grow the red milkweed or bloodflower (Asclepias curassavica) and the white milkweed (Asclepias fruticosa) from seed collected at the roadside. A word about these milkweeds, sometimes called cottonbush: the red one is a native American foodplant for the wanderer or monarch butterfly which is, of course, an émigré American. White milkweed comes from Africa. While not so colourful as its American cousin, its dainty white flowers and unusual seed pods make it a very acceptable garden plant.*

Daisy family*. Erigeron. that prolific little white daisy that can transform a rockery or waste patch in summer—and sometimes spreads rather too willingly—attracts small and medium butterflies. Asters and single dahlias, too, have their adherents, as have the lovely circular flowers of mauve Stokesia. Such typical daisies with cushions of tightly packed disc flowers surrounded by decorative 'petals' are ideal as fast-food counters for insects. This huge family (Asteraceae) includes many flowers attractive to butterflies. Speaking of daisies, it's worth giving some lawn or rockery space to a dandelion or two. The true dandelion (Taraxacum officinale) is not nearly so invasive as the very similar cat's ear (Hypochoeris radicata). You can tell the difference easily—the dandelion has its single flower on sturdy unbranched stems, while the cat's ear has several flowers on a tall, branched stem. And the dandelion 'clock' is whiter and more perfectly globular than the similar but rather spiky one of cat's ear.*

Another weed of the daisy family is the Scotch thistle. In spite of its prickles and tendency to proliferate I consider it worthwhile leaving just one of these to grow to its full 2 metres of flowering stems.

Balsam (or **Impatiens**), an easy-to-grow garden favourite, attracts some butterfly visitors, particularly the red-flowered forms. The single, flat flowers make a convenient platform, and there is plenty of nectar in the spurred tube at the centre.

Viola. A garden is full of surprises and one for me was to see a painted lady butterfly taking a long drink from a purple and white viola. Violas and pansies are favourites but I had not thought of them as butterfly flowers.

Clover. Creamy flowerheads of clover have nectar for smaller butterflies of the family Lycaenidae that spend their days close to the ground. A clover lawn allowed to run to flower is not only attractive but it can be alive with butterflies in summer. The tiny common grass blue, often mistaken for a moth, breeds and feeds on clover.

Bottlebrush (or **Callistemon**) with its stiff, brushlike flower spikes is usually pollinated by nectar-feeding birds like the honeyeaters. Surprisingly, the large red-flowered one in my garden is often visited by the common jezabel butterflies that breed on mistletoe in the bush nearby. The butterflies seem to cope quite well with the long, spiky stamens, pushing their 'tongues' deep into the channels between to suck the nectar.

With the right kind of flowers, the right kind of caterpillar food plants and a little extra care and know-how we can turn every summer into a butterfly summer and add a new dimension of pleasure to days in the garden.

Become a butterfly farmer

Some common butterflies can be reared indoors from either the egg or caterpillar stage. The earlier you take them indoors the less chance of parasitic flies or wasps attacking them. If you start with an egg take the stem and put it in water. A fresh shoot may quickly wither, so be sure to watch for hatching and place the tiny caterpillar carefully onto a new leaf.

If you need to collect a caterpillar, you can best pick it up by bending the leaf down near the head end and 'rolling' the caterpillar onto your finger from underneath. Remember that caterpillars don't have bones, so be careful. Picking one up too firmly *between thumb and finger can damage it. (This applies to butterflies, too – they can lose a lot of loose scales off their wings.)*

If you want to try your hand at raising butterflies, then you need to know something about caterpillar husbandry. Keep your caterpillars on a leafy stem of their proper foodplant in water. Narrow-necked bottles are most suitable as a caterpillar may drown itself in a wide-mouthed vase or jar. When the leaves lose their freshness put a new stem next to the old one. The caterpillar will soon find it and then you can remove the old leaves.

Remember that a caterpillar must moult several times during its life in order to grow. This involves a short quiescent period before the actual casting of the skin, and it's important at this time not to disturb the caterpillar.

When it's fully grown the caterpillar may move away to pupate, so at the later stages a cover is a good idea – transparent so you can watch proceedings. The quiescent pupal period may take weeks or even months so you need to be patient. When the butterfy finally emerges let it sit undisturbed. It needs time to expand its wings. After a while it will drop a lot of fluid – the broken-down, unwanted parts of its caterpillar stages.

When that's all over and the butterfly looks ready, ease your finger under its feet and carry it carefully outside. If it doesn't immediately fly away, let it step onto a leaf to finish preparing itself for flight. There is a lot of pleasure in releasing a new butterfly and seeing how easily it takes to a new life in the sunshine. When you meet it again, feeding on your flowers, you'll feel a sense of kinship with it.

Notes:

Foodplants

Under the descriptions that follow, the butterflies' larval foodplants are divided into 'exotic' and 'native'. Naturally you're more likely to have the exotic plants and trees already growing in your garden or street. But some of the butterflies described have not (yet) taken to using our cultivated plants to breed on.

A few of the butterflies, too, have extremely specialised larval foodplants which makes them unlikely to breed in the average garden. An example is the common jezabel whose caterpillars feed on mistletoe leaves. Then there are the skipper butterflies that feed exclusively on *Lomandra*, a tough, strap-leaved bush plant unlikely to be grown as an ornamental.

Butterflies that breed only on species of wattle or acacia are not such a problem, as our wattles are often grown as landscape and garden subjects. In native gardens, whether natural or planted, many other butterfly foodplants may occur naturally or be obtained from specialist nurseries.

You can obtain information as to whether any of the native plants listed are suitable for gardens from the Society for Growing Australian Plants (SGAPS), an Australia-wide organisation.

If you live close to the bush, those more difficult butterflies may be around anyway, visiting your flower garden year after year for the nectar you so kindly provide for them.

The larval foodplants mentioned with individual butterfly descriptions are also listed separately at the end of this book. They are only a selection of the better-known species.

Nomenclature

In referring to butterflies the words **larva** and **caterpillar** are interchangeable. The juvenile stage of many insects is referred to scientifically as a larva. The word caterpillar is simply the everyday name for the larvae of butterflies and moths.

The **pupa** is the quiescent transitional stage between caterpillar and butterfly. The pupa does not move about or feed. Inside the pupa the final changes take place before the emergence, in due course, of a winged butterfly. Another name for the pupa is chrysalis, but this is tending to go out of use.

The word **exotic** is used for any plant that did not grow naturally in Australia before European settlement but was introduced here as a crop, a garden or street ornamental, or accidentally as a weed.

Distribution

The distribution maps that follow are based on those used in *Butterflies of Australia* by Common and Waterhouse. Any reader wanting a really comprehensive and readable coverage of all Australian butterflies and a more comprehensive list of foodplants could do no better than obtain a copy of this book.

Family Papilionidae *(swallowtails)*

The name 'swallowtail' was originally given to European members of the family because so many of them have a distinct tail to the hindwings. Although only a few of the eighteen Australian species have tails, they include some of our best-known and prettiest, as well as largest, garden butterflies. Most of them are tropical or subtropical.

Papilionid caterpillars have a unique defence against enemies. When disturbed they shoot out from behind their heads a forked organ called an osmeterium. Often brightly coloured, it also produces a pungent smell that may be an effective deterrent against parasitic wasps and flies.

When a swallowtail caterpillar is ready to pupate it attaches itself to a support in two ways. The tip of the abdomen is hooked to a silk pad by a structure at the tip of the abdomen called a cremaster, and just to be on the safe side the body is also supported by a silk girdle fixed around the middle.

When they're feeding at flowers, swallowtail butterflies characteristically hold their wings high and vibrate them – a very pretty sight.

The hindwings of some male swallowtails bear a fringe of scent-bearing hairs along their inner edge. This is normally hidden and only comes into view during courtship when it is used by the male to disperse his scent around the female.

Orchard butterfly *(Princeps aegeus)*

In eastern Australia the orchard swallowtails are among the most common garden visitors, easily recognised in flight by their large size and striking wing patterns.

Courtship of these butterflies is delightful to watch as the male follows close behind the female, fanning her with his wings to disperse his scent around her. This identifies him to the female as a potential mate. If she is uncommitted she will indicate acceptance, and mating may go on for an hour or more.

Larval foodplants
Exotic: Citrus trees of backyard and orchard – orange, lemon, grapefruit, etc. (family Rutaceae).

Native: Many members of the Rutaceae family, some of which are cultivated as garden shrubs (*Eriostemon,* for example).

Butterfly stages
Egg: Round, creamy yellow, usually laid singly under young leaves at the tip of a stem.

Larva: Rather humped in front, tapering to the rear. At first glistening brown and white, easily taken for a bird dropping when at rest. Intermediate stage mottled olive green with several brown diagonal bands and a white border low down on either side. Later bright green with whitish diagonal bands and edging.

Pupa: Colour varies from green to pinky brown or grey-brown, blending so well with the texture of stem or branch it is difficult to locate.

Adult: Large. Male and female: basically black and white with red and blue markings, female with paler forewings and more colour on the hindwings.

Distribution map

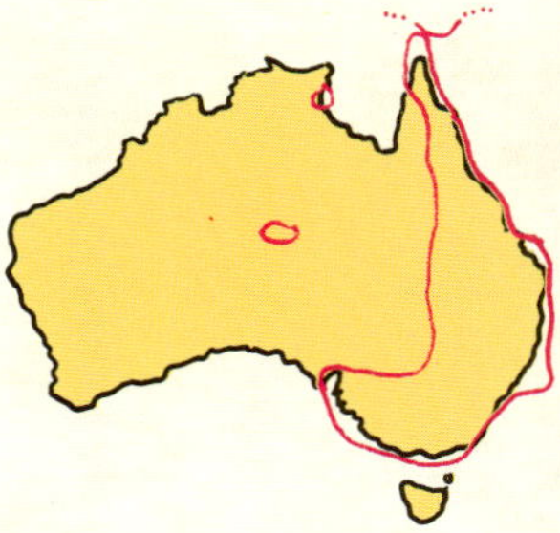

Male

Female

Ulysses butterfly *(Princeps ulysses joesa)*

It is impossible to confuse these glorious butterflies with any other. They are generally seen around rainforest, flying high with blue wings flickering, or feeding at forest edges on such flowers as lantana. The males will fly down to investigate any blue objects such as clothing. Ulysses butterflies will visit gardens reasonably close to rainforest where nectar-rich flowers are grown.

Larval foodplants
Exotic: Possibly on cultivated citrus (orange, lemon, etc.).
Native: Include tropical rainforest trees *Euodia elleryana* and *Euodia bonwickii* (family Rutaceae), especially tender, young regrowth.

Butterfly stages
Egg: Round, pale green or yellow, usually laid on new leaves.

Larva: At first green with blue, orange and white markings and short, dark spines, with longer white spines front and rear. When mature, stout and rather tapered towards rear, green with a single pair of white, fleshy spines at the 'tail' and a pair or several pairs of white blotches above.

Pupa: As in photograph, but colour ranges from green to light brown with an orange or pinkish tinge.

Adult: Large. Male: (above) brilliant metallic blue with wide, black borders; (below) dark brown with lighter brown patches and a series of orange to orange-brown spots around border of hindwing. Female: similar but with smaller blue areas and somewhat duller black borders.

Distribution map

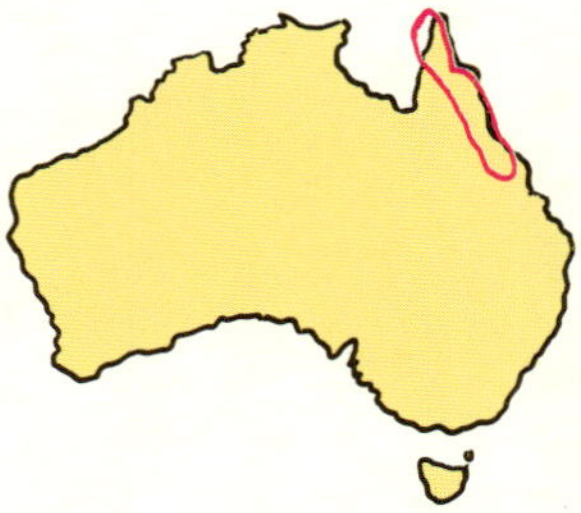

Male

Dingy swallowtail *(Eleppone anactus)*

In spite of their uncomplimentary name, these pretty butterflies are far from dingy. Normal flight is a slow glide-and-flutter but they can make a quick getaway if chased. Because they breed on cultivated citrus, dingy swallowtails are common around gardens and orchards that provide them.

Larval foodplants
Exotic: Sometimes known as the lesser orchard butterfly, this one also feeds on oranges and other cultivated citrus in backyards and orchards.

Native: All the native foodplants belong to the family Rutaceae and include species of *Eremocitrus* and *Microcitrus.*

Butterfly stages
Egg: Round, pale yellow, laid singly on young leaves of the foodplant.

Larva: Black at first with a number of short spines. More bluish black when mature, with rows of yellow spots down the back and along the sides.

Pupa: Slenderer than orchard swallowtail but similar in texture; a pair of projections at head end. Colour is variable in shades of green, brown and grey, or mixed.

Adult: Medium size. Both sexes coloured somewhat like female orchard swallowtail but smaller and with narrower front wings.

Distribution map

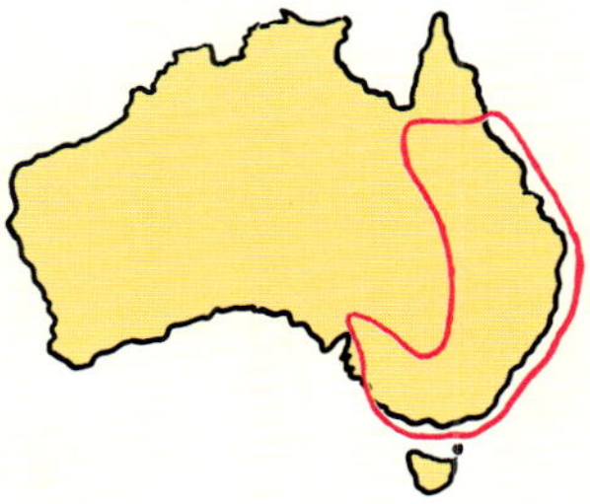

Female

Chequered swallowtail *(Princeps demoleus)*

While chequered swallowtails are widespread on mainland Australia, including inland, they are not common along the south-east coast. The butterflies usually fly low and feed at herbaceous flowers, including crops, wayside weeds and garden plants.

Larval foodplants
Exotic: Larvae have been successfully reared on the garden shrub *Psoralea pinnata* and on citrus trees. Outside Australia, citrus species are common foodplants for this widespread butterfly.

Native: All known native foodplants are various species of *Psoralea*. This swallowtail is exceptional in feeding on a member of the pea family (Fabaceae).

Butterfly stages
Egg: Round, yellow.

Larva: Early stage black with black spines, later stages with orange patches along sides. Green or yellowish when mature, with black, orange and white patterns and paired short spines front and back.

Pupa: Green or brown with darker markings.

Adult: Medium to large. Male and Female: dark brownish black above with lacy pattern of cream spots and patches and large orange spot on the hindwing. Similar below but paler, hindwing with several large brownish orange 'eyespots'.

Distribution map

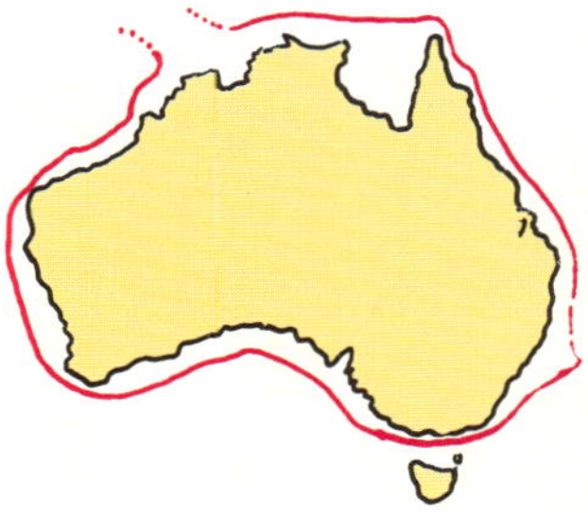

Male

Birdwing butterfly *(Troides priamus)*

The size and characteristic sailing flight of these lovely butterflies make them recognisable even high in the canopy. But they readily come down to feed on roadside lantana, and are fairly common visitors to tropical gardens. Male birdwings will regularly patrol their territories watching for females and chasing off other butterflies.

Larval foodplants
Native: Exclusively species of *Aristolochia*, tropical rainforest vines closely related to the familiar garden exotic Dutchman's pipe.

Butterfly stages
Egg: Large, round, laid singly on or near foodplant.

Larva: Thickset, somewhat tapered to rear. At first nearly black or very dark reddish with short spines and hairs. Later smoky brown or purple with a series of pinkish fleshy spines and a conspicuous pair of white spines about midway centre.

Pupa: Stout, golden yellow or ochre.

Adult: Male and female very different, female larger. Male: forewing velvety black with emerald green markings, hindwing blue-green suffused with yellow and patterned with several black spots. Female: forewing black with white bands and blotches, hindwing black with outer half patterned black on yellow and white.

Distribution map

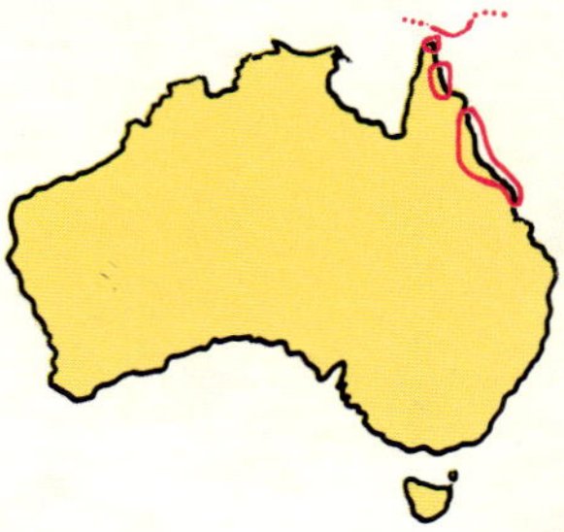

Male

Blue triangle *(Graphium sarpedon choredon)*

Blue triangles are common and widespread Australian swallowtails and belong to a group known as the kite butterflies from the shape of their wings. Blue triangles will often congregate on the ground in damp places to drink taking in water at one end and periodically squirting it out at the other. They are easy and rewarding to rear indoors.

Larval foodplants
Exotic: Camphor laurel trees (*Cinnamomum camphora*) in New South Wales and southern Queensland.

Native: These belong mainly to the laurel family (Lauraceae), with others in the Monimaceae and Sapotaceae.

Butterfly stages
Egg: Round, yellowish or greenish, laid singly on young leaves.

Larva: Nearly black on hatching, later olive to bright green; smooth, humped in front, tapered to rear. Rests on the upper surface of leaves on pad of silk; moves with jerky action. Can be located by chewing sound when feeding, or by strong scent of yellow osmeterium if disturbed.

Pupa: Pale green with distinct veins and a large projecting 'horn', usually suspended under leaf. When about to emerge the skin becomes transparent and the blue and black colours of the butterfly are clearly visible. Often parasitised by flies, in which case irregular dark spots appear.

Adult: Male and female are similar in colour; distinctive in flight, not easily confused with any other medium-sized butterfly.

Female

Distribution map

Female

Macleay's swallowtail

(Graphium macleayanum)

Less common near coast than in uplands where great numbers congregate in summer, feeding, mating and laying eggs. Males fly around summits of mountains in an activity called 'hilltopping'. They visit gardens and, like the closely related blue triangle, will breed readily on camphor laurel where available. This is the only swallowtail butterfly found in Tasmania.

Larval foodplants
Exotic: Camphor laurel (family Lauraceae).

Native: Various plants of the families Lauraceae, Winteraceae, Monimaceae and Rutaceae.

Butterfly stages
Egg: Round, yellowish, laid singly usually (but not always) on new shoots of the foodplant.

Larva: Rather similar in shape to blue triangle larva. Olive green at first with black hairs and tubercles. Later speckled darker green or yellowish brown. When mature, green with tiny pale dots, pale bluish beneath, rather humped in front with two pairs of small spines and a reddish bar.

Pupa: Speckled green or yellowish, with projection near front; usually suspended under a leaf.

Adult: Medium size. Male and female: above pale green and whitish with wide black borders. Below richer green with wide borders of brown and black and paler decorations. Hindwings have narrow clubbed tails.

Distribution map

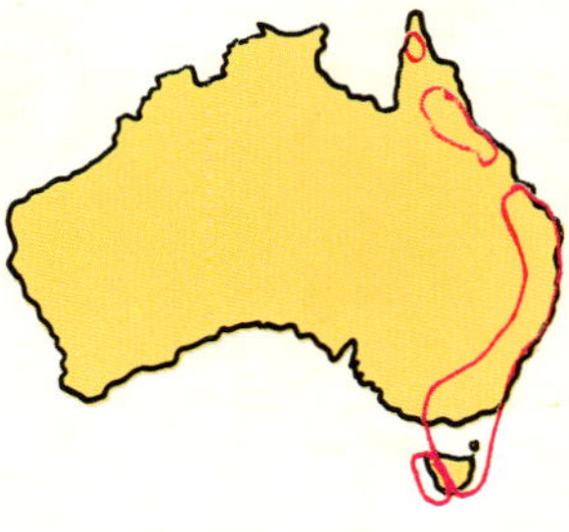

Female

Family Nymphalidae *(nymphs, browns and danaids)*

This large and diverse family includes many medium-sized, brown-patterned butterflies common in gardens, and some striking black and white species. Butterflies of this family have the front pair of legs so short they are useless for walking and are usually held close against the body.

Nymphalid caterpillars vary enormously in form, colour and skin texture. They pupate without a supporting girdle, simply hanging by the cremaster.

Most of the better known nymphalids are included in three major subfamilies:

The browns (subfamily Satyrinae) *tend to be shade lovers and rather weak flyers. They're not so often seen at flowers as some other butterflies but are nevertheless common in gardens because they breed on grasses.*

The *nymphs* (subfamily Nymphalinae) *are rapid flyers and like to 'sunbathe' with wings spread, often on open ground. Some are attracted to sweet fruit juice as well as nectar. The fermented sap of trees is relished and a butterfly that's been on it for a while may be easily approached.*

The *danaids* (subfamily Danainae), *sometimes called milkweed butterflies, prefer strong sunlight. Most are unpalatable to birds due to the toxins they ingest with their foodplants. Males of several species have a pair of scented 'pompoms' (hair pencils) tucked away at the tip of the abdomen, which they produce with striking effect during courtship.*

Common brown *(Heteronympha merope merope)*

In Sydney gardens, males of this butterfly are commonly flying around before the females are seen. Mating takes place in spring but eggs are not laid until autumn when males have disappeared. At rest on the ground the butterflies of both sexes are well camouflaged, and are most often seen taking flight when disturbed.

Larval foodplants
Exotic: Various grasses (usually family Poaceae).

Native: Various grasses (family Poaceae) including *Themeda australis* (kangaroo grass).

Butterfly stages
Egg: Cream.

Larva: Rear end forked. Early stage green with black head and long black hairs, later green with paler stripes, head black with black hairs. When mature may be green, grey or mottled brown, densely covered with short bristles, head brown.

Pupa: Grey or brown with darker markings; found on the ground among debris or overhanging grass or herbs.

Adult: Male: brown, bordered and patterned very dark brown, a small blue-centred eyespot on each wing; below pale brown, some black on forewing, eyespots as above. Female: larger, brighter; above orange and black with yellow patches on forewing, eyespots as in male; below forewing as above but lighter brown tip, hindwing light brown.

Distribution map

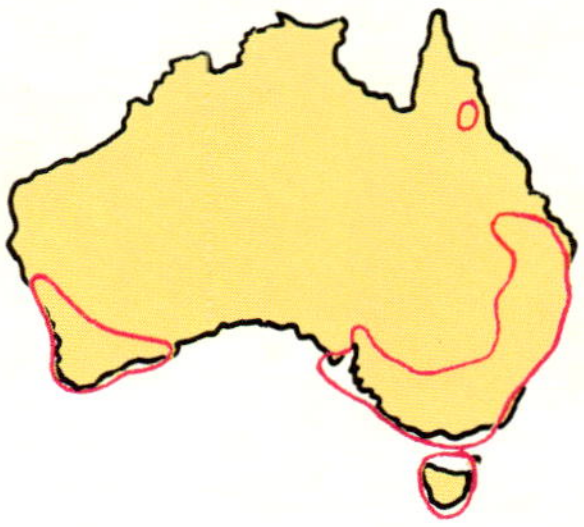

Male

Female

Common brown ringlet

(Hypocysta metirius)

These are quite common but inconspicuous, keeping low to the ground and feeding at small flowers. Their small size and the eyespots on the hindwings help to identify this and several other members of the 'ringlet' group.

Larval foodplants
Exotic: *Cynodon dactylon* (couch grass) and probably others.

Native: Common grasses, including *Imperata* (blady grass).

Butterfly stages
Egg: Pale green.

Larva: Rear end forked; green with small white spots; distinct head with two short pink-tipped horns.

Pupa: Brown, suspended head down.

Adult: Small, with distinctly pointed forewings. Male: above dark brown, hindwing with large orange patch and prominent eyespot; below pale brownish with eyespots on hindwing. Female: similar but paler.

Distribution map

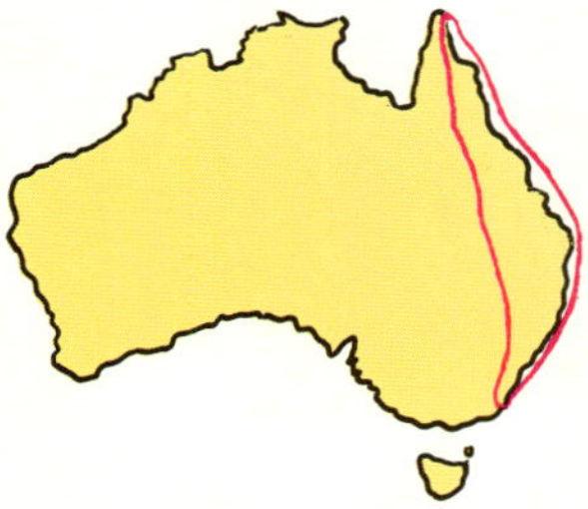

Female

Swordgrass brown *(Tisiphone abeona)*

These are fairly large, sombrely handsome butterflies, often encountered daily in the same areas where they patrol a territory. They fly low, settling on the ground where they are difficult to locate.

Larval foodplants
Native: Swordgrass, which is a species of *Gahnia* (family Cyperaceae).

Butterfly stages
Egg: Large, bright green or some shade of green, laid singly on young shoots of foodplant or older leaves drooping close to the ground.

Larva: Rear end forked; bright or yellowish green with paler longitudinal stripes. At first with black head and sparse long hairs. Later densely covered with tiny bristles rising from white dots; may have a reddish brown band across back, head pale green.

Pupa: Smooth, rather stout, bright green or some shade of green; wings show bright yellow outline; suspended head down under drooping leaves of foodplant or on nearby plant.

Adult: Male: both surfaces of both wings rich dark brown; forewing above with bright orange band and two blue eyespots, below similar but paler; hindwing above with large blue and orange eyespot, below with one large and one smaller eyespot and several white or pale lines. Female: similar but paler.

Distribution map

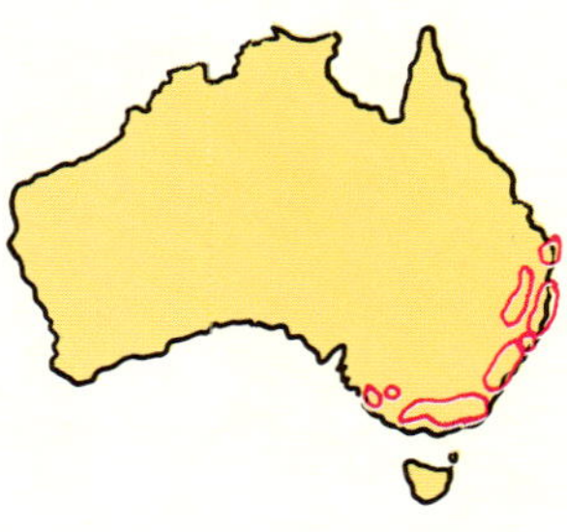

Female (left) and male

Female (left) and male (right)

Evening brown *(Melanitis leda bankia)*

The larvae of these butterflies can be found feeding during the day but blend well with the leaf blades in spite of their distinctive headgear. The fairly large adults are on the wing mainly at dusk and dawn, avoiding sunlight. They spend much time on the ground with wings closed, flying only short distances if disturbed.

Larval foodplants
Exotic: Coarse grasses (family Poaceae) including paspalum, buffalo grass, millet and sugarcane.

Native: Coarse native grasses, including blady grass (*Imperata*).

Butterfly stages
Larva: Rear end forked, green or yellowish green, covered with very short hairs rising from white dots; easy to recognise by the distinct head with a reddish brown stripe on each side, and bearing a pair of reddish brown, hairy 'horns'.

Pupa: Smooth, plain green, suspended head down on foodplant.

Adult: Male and female: upper surface of wings diffuse chestnut to dusky brown; two white-centred black spots on each wing, more obvious in female. Underside of wings cryptically dead-leaf brown.

Distribution map

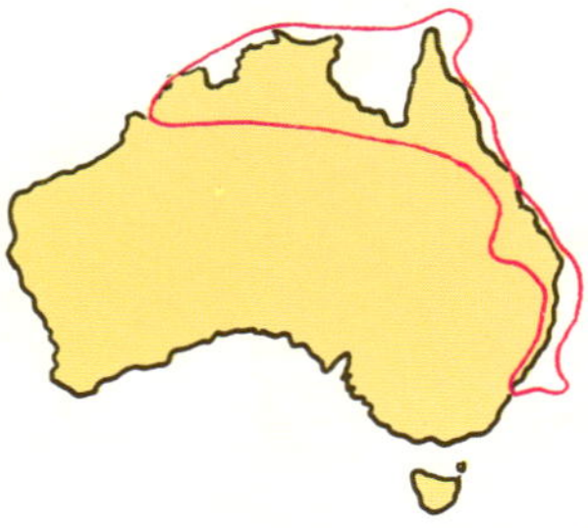

Male

Australian painted lady *(Vanessa kershawi)*

These very attractive nymph butterflies are often common around garden flowerbeds in spring and summer. They alight with wings half open to feed on the nectar of low-growing flowers or rest between meals on sunny paths and rockeries. They are rapid and tireless flyers, known to make migratory flights southward in spring.

Larval foodplants
Exotic: Plants of the daisy family (Asteraceae) including capeweed, Scotch thistle, cudweed and artemisia. Reported to have bred on garden lavender in Canberra.

Native: A number of plants of the daisy family.

Butterfly stages
Egg: Rather higher than wide, translucent green with vertical ribs, laid singly on foodplant.

Larva: Variable in colour, shades of brown or yellowish grey or green with paler stripe along top and sides and numerous short, branched spines.

Pupa: Angular in shape with several projections; variable in colour with darker markings, often with silver or gold spots.

Adult: Male and Female: medium-sized, with wings strikingly patterned in black, orange, brown and white; paler below.

Distribution map

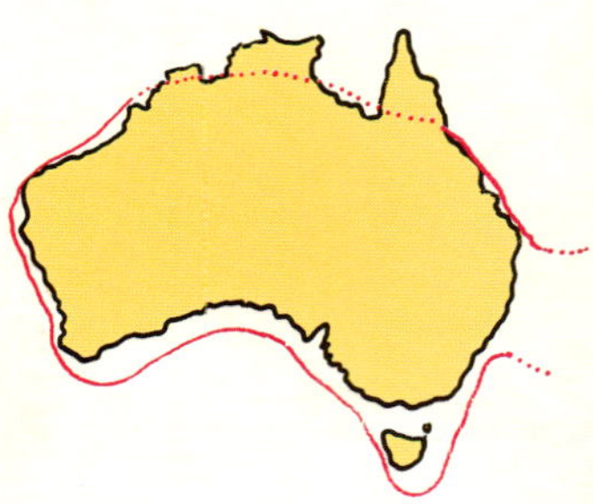

Male

Female

Australian admiral *(Vanessa itea)*

The habits of this pretty butterfly resemble those of the painted lady. These butterflies are strongly attracted to fermented sap flowing from trees and will feed there for long periods with wings usually closed.

Larval foodplants
Exotic: Stinging nettle (*Urtica urens*), a member of the Urticaceae family.

Native: Australian stinging nettle, *Urtica incisa*.

Butterfly stages
Egg: Domed, green, strongly ribbed, laid singly or more often in pairs on foodplant.

Larva: Shades of brown, greyish green or yellow with paler stripes on top and along sides. They feed at night, hiding by day among leaves which may be joined together with silk threads.

Pupa: Variable, some shade of brown with darker markings, may have silver or gold spots.

Adult: Somewhat similar to its close relative, the painted lady, but readily distinguished by the broad, pale yellow band on both surfaces of the front wings.

Distribution map

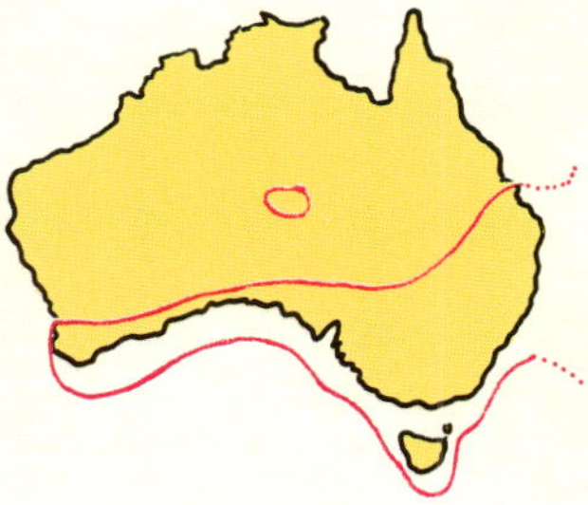

Female

Meadow argus *(Junonia villida)*

The third of a trio of attractive and widespread nymphs, this butterfly has much the same habits as the painted lady. Flitting quickly from flower to flower for nectar, it often rests in the sun with wings spread wide – a bonus for nature photographers as most butterflies rest with wings folded.

Larval foodplants
Exotic: Garden plants and wildings of several families, including snapdragon, verbena, portulaca, purple top and plantain.

Native: Plants of a number of genera including *Goodenia* and *Scaevola* (family Goodeniaceae).

Butterfly stages
Egg: Domed, green, slightly higher than wide, with vertical ribs and less obvious horizontal ribs, laid singly on foodplant.

Larva: Black with many short, thick, branched spines; head black with short hairs and pair of branched black spines. These caterpillars feed openly by day or night and can sometimes be seen lying on a leaf or on the ground near the base of the foodplant in full sunshine.

Pupa: Dull, rather rough textured with a few small knobs; patchy dark and light brown or whitish; attached to plant by hooks at tail end.

Male

Adult: Male and Female: wings above as in photograph; below, forewing paler, hindwing pale without obvious eyespots.

Distribution map

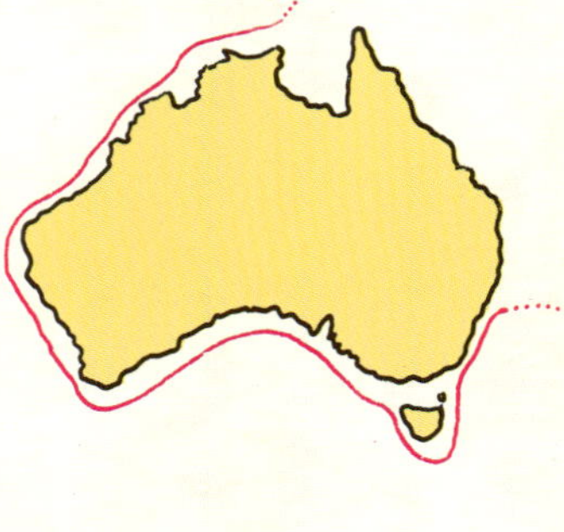

Tailed emperor *(Polyura sempronius)*

A strikingly unusual caterpillar and a handsome butterfly. The butterflies rest head downward with wings closed, often high up in trees. They are best approached when preoccupied (and perhaps slightly befuddled) drinking at a patch of fermented sap on a tree-trunk. Easy and rewarding to rear on cut foodplants indoors – if you can detect the surprisingly well-camouflaged larvae.

Butterfly stages

Egg: Round, yellowish, laid singly on upper surface of leaf.

Larva: Distinctive, as illustrated; when newly hatched more yellowish with only two pairs of 'horns'. Well camouflaged on foodplants.

Pupa: Fat, shiny, green with white patterns, suspended by tail on foodplant.

Larval foodplants

Exotic: Include crepe myrtle (*Lagerstroemia indica*), elm (*Ulmus* spp.), false acacia (*Robinia pseudoacacia*), camphor laurel (*Cinnamomum camphora*), poinciana (*Delonix regia*), golden-rain tree (*Cassia fistula*), candlestick cassia (*C. alata*) and bird-of-paradise shrub (*Caesalpinia gilliesii*).

Native: Main foodplants are wattles (*Acacia*), both feathery and plain-leaved species; for example, Cootamundra wattle (*A. baileyana*) and Queensland wattle (*A. podalyriifolia*). Native foodplants also include kurrajong (*Brachychiton populneus*) and the crested wattle (*Albizzia lophantha*), the latter being native to Western Australia but introduced and naturalised elsewhere.

Adult: Male and Female: fairly large; creamy white above with black markings; below brightly patterned in shades of brown. A pair of short tails on hindwings.

Distribution map

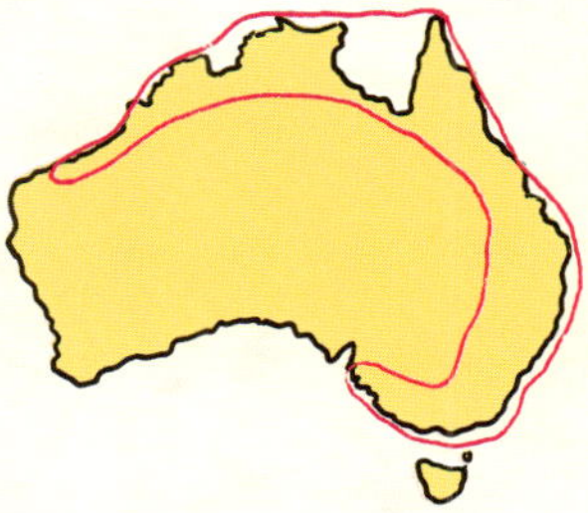

Female

Male

Common eggfly *(Hypolimnas bolina)*

A common visitor in tropical and subtropical gardens and even around well-watered outback properties; less common in the south of its range. The large white spots on the male's wings show a striking colour change to bright blue or purple when viewed at certain angles. This is easily observed as the butterfly commonly rests with wings spread.

Larval foodplants
Exotic: Include Ganges bluebell (*Asystasia gangetica*), *Polygonum prostratum* and *Portulaca* spp.

Native: Most common are joyweed (*Alternanthera denticulata*) and Paddy's lucerne (*Sida rhombifolia*) which are native weeds of cultivation. Also certain plants of the families Amaranthaceae, Malvaceae, Acanthaceae, Portulacaceae, Polygonaceae, Rubiaceae and Asteraceae.

Butterfly stages
Egg: Yellowish turning green, vertically ribbed. In batches under leaves of foodplant.

Larva: At first dark green with shiny black head, later dark brown or black with yellow stripe along sides and branched spines; head orange-brown with two long black bristly spines.

Pupa: Brown, mottled darker.

Distribution map

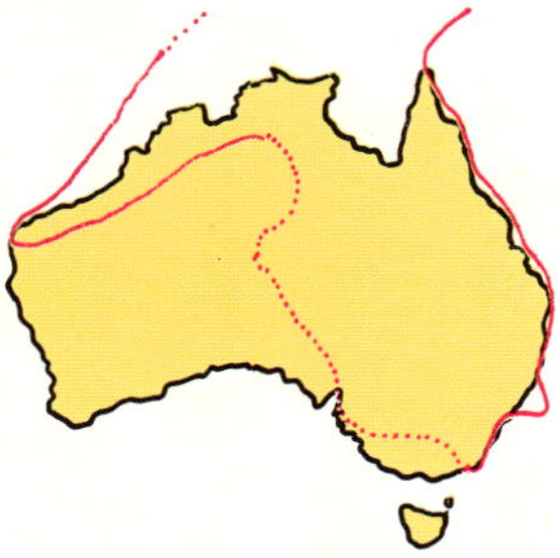

Male

Adult: Male and Female: very different above, as illustrated; somewhat similar below, brown flushed orange with white and bluish spots and patches. Female larger.

Female

Wanderer *(Danaus plexippus)*

An immigrant from America and now one of 'our' most common and attractive species. Unlike many introduced animals the wanderer does no harm to natives or garden plants because of its special food preferences. Wanderers probably reached our shores thousands of years ago but were unable to settle here until we had introduced their foodplants. Milkweeds, now wayside wildings, make attractive garden subjects and can be grown from collected seed. There is no surer way of attracting these beautiful butterflies.

Larval foodplants
Exotic: Species of milkweed from Africa (*Asclepias fruticosa* and *A. rotundifolia*) and from America (*Asclepias curassavica*). The moth plant (*Araujia hortorum*), a creeper from South America often growing in waste places is sometimes listed as a foodplant though I have not found it a successful one.

Butterfly stages
Egg: Tall, creamy yellow, laid singly but often in numbers on buds, shoots or under leaves of foodplant.

Larva: Banded black and yellow with two long, black, fleshy filaments in front and a shorter pair at the rear. Can be seen feeding freely in daylight as plant toxins acceptable to them are irritant to vertebrate predators such as birds.

Pupa: Jade green with a band of golden spots towards the head end, suspended head down usually not on the foodplant but nearby.

Adult: Male and Female: above rich tawny orange with black veins; below paler. Males can be identified by a prominent black 'sex mark' on each hindwing.

Distribution map

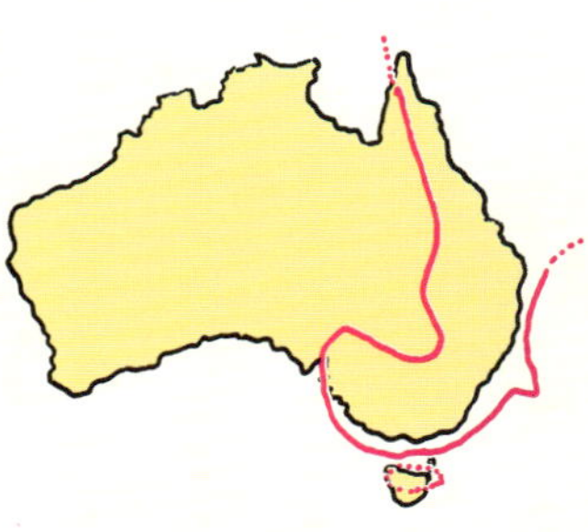

Male

Common Australian crow or Oleander butterfly *(Euploea core corinna*

Male crow butterflies can produce from the tip of the abdomen a remarkable structure like a pompom of bright yellow hairs. Called a hair pencil, it is used to disperse a scent or pheromone over the female during courtship. This is often expanded if the butterfly is captured and held.

Larval foodplants
Exotic: Oleander (*Nerium oleander*), Chilean jasmine (*Mandevillea laxa*), star jasmine (*Trachelospermum jasminoides*), *Stephanotis* spp., milkweeds (*Asclepias* spp.)

Native: Include species of fig (*Ficus*), *Hoya australis, Leichhardtia australis.*

Butterfly stages
Egg: Much higher than wide, pale yellow, laid singly on leaves of foodplant.

Larva: At first greenish with short dark hairs, later pale brown with black head and four pairs of short fleshy filaments. Mature larva orange-brown banded black and white, with four pairs of long fleshy filaments.

Pupa: Unmistakable, shining metallic silver or gold, sometimes with brown markings, suspended head down.

Adult: Male and female: very dark brown above with fine white spots along outer margins and a series of larger white spots; below similar but paler.

Distribution map

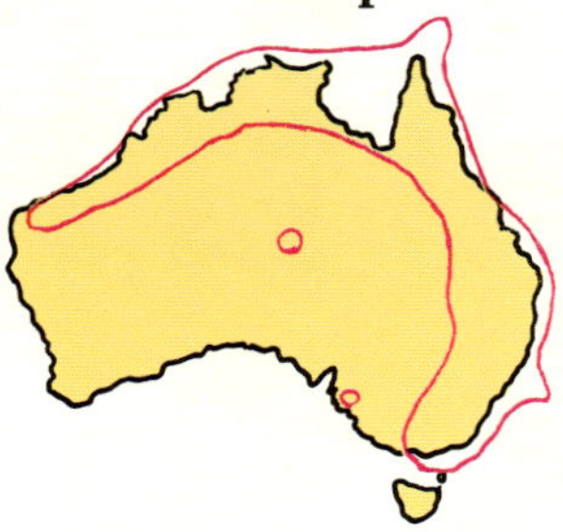

Female

Family Pieridae *(whites and yellows)*

Most of the medium-sized, mainly white and yellow butterflies we see around belong to this family. While not spectacular these sun-lovers add a touch of lightness to the garden scene. They settle immediately a cloud crosses the sun but they're up and about again as soon as the shadow passes.

The larvae of pierid butterflies are 'typical' caterpillars, slender and cylindrical, without fleshy spines or long hairs. The pupae are supported by a cremaster and a girdle.

This family includes the attractive and interesting genus Delias, *generally known as mistletoe butterflies. As the name implies, their larvae feed only on mistletoe foliage, and it's usually high in the treetops where mistletoe grows that you see the butterflies on the wing.*

Mistletoe butterflies are exceptionally colourful for this family, and they're unusual in having the brightest colours, such as red, underneath the wings. The strong colour pattern below contrasting with the pure white above give these butterflies a characteristic flickering flight.

Migrants and grass yellows are related groups that can be confusing when they're on the wing or feeding, particularly as migrant females can vary in colour. However, migrants are quite large and strong flyers while the much smaller grass yellows fly erratically and usually closer to the ground.

The most common pierid butterfly in gardens is unfortunately the European cabbage white (*Pieris rapae*), a pest species we'd be better off without. The caterpillars simply love cabbage, cauliflower, turnip and related vegetables and, in the flower garden, nasturtiums.

Common grass yellow *(Eurema hecabe phoebus)*

In the tropics this widespread butterfly is familiar in gardens throughout the year; farther south it is a summer and autumn species. This one represents a number of very similar species of 'grass yellow' butterflies, occurring mainly in tropical and eastern States. Most appear to include species of Cassia among their foodplants.

Larval foodplants
Native: Include many species of *Breynia, Acacia, Indigofera* and native and garden species of *Cassia*.

Butterfly stages

Egg: White, laid singly on foodplant.

Larva: Green with narrow stripe along sides, hard to detect when at rest.

Pupa: Narrow, green; attached by rear end and silk girdle to underside of leaf.

Adult: Male: small to medium-sized; above yellow with black borders; below yellow with variable dark markings. Female: similar but paler.

Distribution map

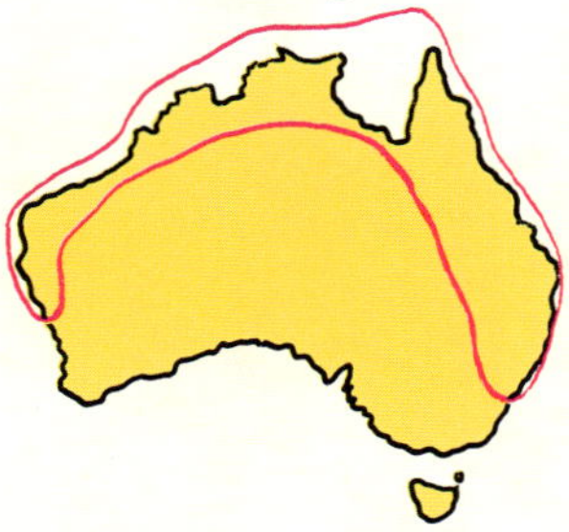

Lemon migrant *(Catopsilia pomona)*

Common in central and northern parts of their range, particularly around tropical towns where the exotic Cassia fistula is a common garden tree.

Distribution map

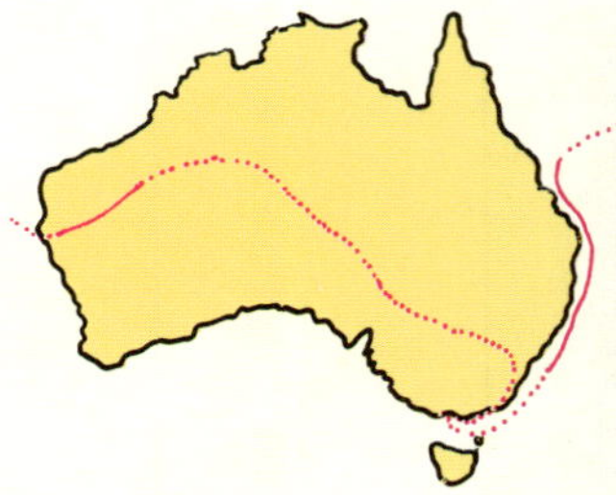

Larval foodplants
Exotic: Include *Cassia fistula* (golden-rain tree) and *Cassia nodosa* (pink-and-white shower).

Native: Many species of *Cassia.*

Butterfly stages
Egg: White to pale yellow, three times higher than wide.

Larva: Long and slender when mature; back dark green with cream and black lateral stripes. Hard to detect when resting on midrib of leaf.

Pupa: Pale green with a whitish stripe, wings forming a keel in front; attached to underside of cassia leaflet by 'tail' and silk girdle.

Adult: Male and female: medium to small. Colour variable, ranging from cream to lemon yellow, female with some black markings on forewing and sometimes a reddish blotch under hindwing. Antennae may be pink or black.

Female

Caper white *(Anaphaeis java teutonia)*

Caper whites are very common butterflies. In spite of their restricted food preferences they are widespread and frequently seen because of their migratory habits. At times they take flight in their thousands, moving into southern areas where their foodplants are not known to grow.

Larval foodplants
Native: Trees and shrubs of genus *Capparis* (or capers); also, in central and northern New South Wales, *Apophyllum anomalum*, a broom-like shrub of the same family (Capparaceae).

Male

Distribution map

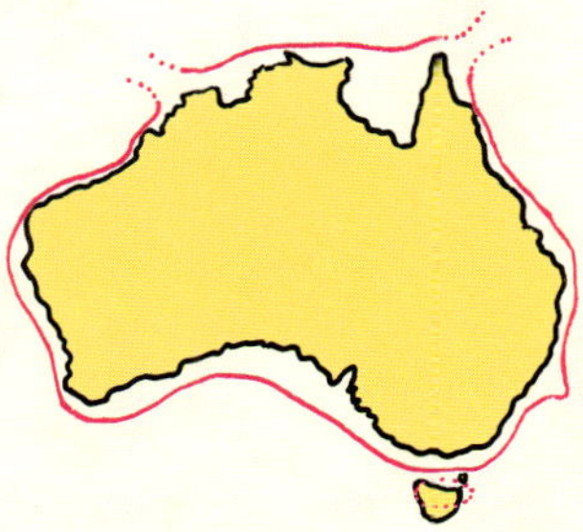

Male

Butterfly stages

Egg: White becoming yellow; twice as high as wide with strong vertical and finer horizontal ribs, laid in great numbers on leaves of the foodplant.

Larva: Mature larva brown to olive green with white hairs rising from yellow dots.

Pupa: Matt in texture, a pair of projections about midway; pale with black blotches and sometimes small golden spots, attached by rear end and silk girdle.

Adult: Male: above white, black outer edges with some white markings; below patterned black and orange on white. Female (light form): similar but with additional black markings above. Female (dark form): above white strongly bordered black; below, patterned with orange and black.

Common albatross *(Appias paulina ega)*

Often seen in great numbers flying around larval foodplants.

Larval foodplants
Native: *Drypetes australasica.* Related *Appias* species from the Orient feed on *Capparis* spp.

Butterfly stages
Larva: Grey-green with raised black spots and white line along back; head yellow with black spots.

Pupa: Matt in texture; several spines jutting sideways and at head end a long, narrow, upward-curving spine with a black tip. Attached by rear end and silk girdle.

Adult: Male: white above with black markings on tip of forewing; below forewing yellow and white with two dark brown spots, hindwing yellow, but colour varies. Female: white above, forewing with black and white apex, hindwing with black border; below white and yellow, forewing with black and pinkish brown apex, hindwing with wide pinkish brown border.

Distribution map

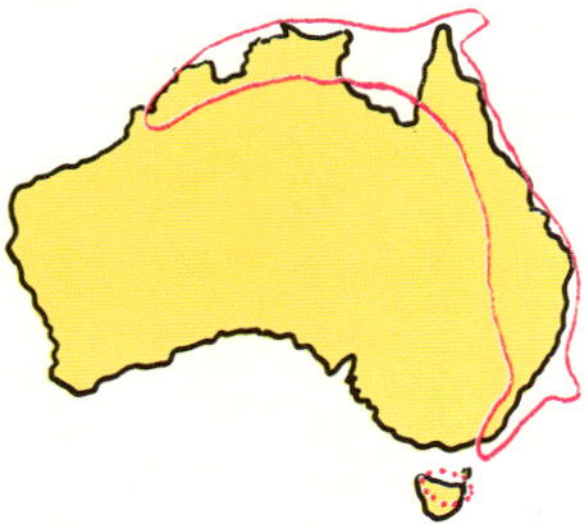

Male

Male

Cabbage white *(Pieris rapae)*

This European butterfly was accidentally introduced to Australia in 1937 and is now widespread, especially in the more temperate southern States but also in north Queensland and central Australia. Unlike most of our native butterflies, the cabbage white is a pest of home and market gardens and not to be encouraged!

Larval foodplants
Exotic: Include vegetables of the Brassicaceae family – cabbage, cauliflower, broccoli, turnip, mustard and radish – and also the garden plants nasturtium, mignonette and spider flower (*Cleome*).

Butterfly stages
Egg: Cream or yellowish, tall, laid singly on foodplant.

Larva: Velvety green with light stripe along back.

Pupa: Green to yellowish brown or grey depending on situation; may be on foodplant or adjacent plant or object; attached by cremaster and sling.

Adult: Medium to small. Male: above forewing white with one or two small black blotches and greyish dusting, hindwing with one black spot; below forewing whitish yellow with two black blotches, hindwing smoky yellowish. Female: similar but creamy white above with blotches on forewing more distinct.

Distribution map

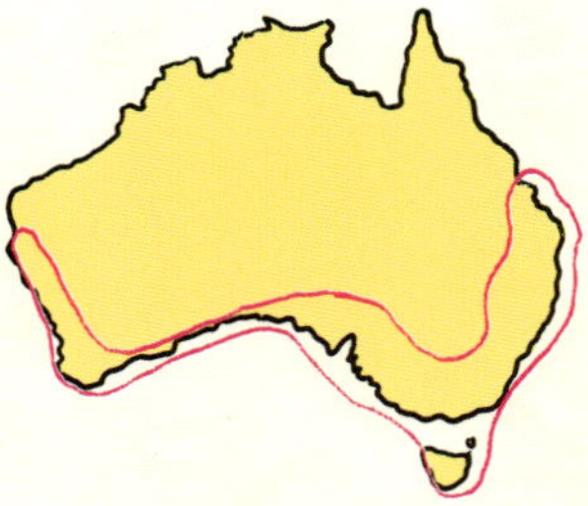

Female

Common jezabel *(Delias nigrina)*

One of the 'mistletoe butterflies', a group of attractive butterflies that breed almost exclusively (with one exception) on plants of the mistletoe family. The exception is the wood white which feeds also on native cherry (species of Exocarpus) and Santalum. The foodplants are not in cultivation but the butterflies are commonly seen in bushland adjacent to gardens and will visit flowers, particularly lantana and natives such as bottlebrush.

The common jezabel is typical of the group and is often very common, even in winter.

Larval foodplants
Native: Mistletoes (family Loranthaceae), including *Amyema congener* (on *Casuarina, Acacia* and *Geijera*, etc.), *Muellerina eucalyptoides* (usually on *Eucalyptus* but also on some exotic trees), *M. celastroides* (usually on *Casuarina* and *Banksia*).

Butterfly stages
Egg: Yellow, in patches on the mistletoe.

Larva: Dark brown or olive, rows of white hairs from yellow bases; head black with white hairs.

Pupa: Orange yellow with black ridge and spines, may be singly on foodplant or adjacent, sometimes beneath host tree near ground.

Adult: Male: above white, apex of forewing black with series of white spots; below mostly black, forewing with row of yellow spots across apex, hindwing with circle of red spots. Female: as male above but greyish white, both wings widely bordered black; below similar to male.

Distribution map

Male

Wood white *(Delias aganippe)*

Another of the 'mistletoe' group, this is the only member that doesn't breed exclusively on mistletoe. It is a common butterfly in southern States, seen perhaps more readily because of its range of foodplants. It is not unusual when travelling inland to see great numbers of these butterflies emerging and fluttering around isolated bushes of native cherry and Santalum.

Larval foodplants
Native: Mistletoes (family Loranthaceae), mainly species of *Amyema*, and also members of the Santalaceae family, for example, species of *Exocarpus* (native cherry) and *Santalum*.

Butterfly stages
Egg: Orange-yellow, in large batches on foodplant.

Larva: Very dark, with raised white spots and white hairs.

Pupa: Dark brown and white, ridged, with blunt projections above. Often in great and conspicuous numbers, attached anywhere on foodplant or in vicinity, often at some distance.

Adult: Male: dusky white above, black borders spotted white, some black markings; below strongly patterned black, white and yellow with conspicuous scarlet spots bordering hindwing. Female: similar but whiter above.

Distribution map

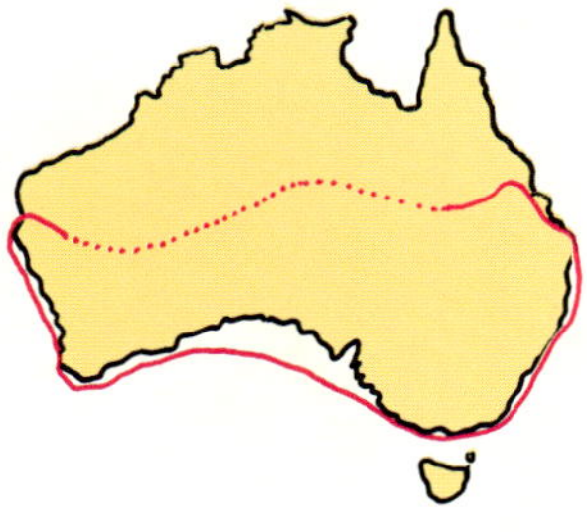

Female

This Imperial white (male) is another of the mistletoe butterflies closely related to the wood white.

Family Lycaenidae *(blues and coppers)*

These are the small jewels of the butterfly world – but not the easiest to see and admire, let alone photograph. Most of them wear their brilliant metallic colours on the upper surface of the wings, with undersides so well camouflaged they are almost invisible when at rest. Most are fast on the wing and quick to take flight when approached.

Even the larvae of these butterflies are different. Many are oval in outline, rather the shape of a woodlouse, with the head hidden. Some are prettily coloured and patterned in shades of brown or green, others plain dark brown to black. The pupae are supported by a girdle and while there is no special cremaster, a set of anal hooks performs the same function.

Nearly all lycaenid larvae are attended by ants. The ants are attracted by drops of sweet fluid produced by special glands, in particular a

central gland towards the rear which can be seen to produce drops of fluid when stimulated by the ants. The benefits are mutual, as the ants provide the larvae with protection just by being with them.

In some lycaenid species, such as the imperial blue, small black ants simply visit the larvae on the acacias while they're feeding. At the other end of the scale, the larvae of certain mistletoe-feeding lycaenids actually live as guests in the nests of sugar ants. The ants accompany the larvae on their nightly journeys to and from the mistletoes they feed on.

Many common lycaenid butterflies are small and unobtrusive. We see them around our gardens all the time, and sometimes mistake them for little grey-blue or brownish moths. But these are daytime flyers and, on a closer look, unmistakably butterflies.

Common grass blue (Zizina labradus)

This is probably our most common garden butterfly, usually seen fluttering around lawns where clover is allowed to grow. In spite of their numbers they are only a minor pest on introduced plants.

Larval foodplants
Exotic: Low-growing plants of the Fabaceae family, including clover, lucerne, garden bean, garden pea and broad bean. In gardens usually on clover.

Native: Low-growing legumes of the Fabaceae family, including the genera *Glycine, Desmodium, Indigofera, Psoralea* and *Lotus.*

Butterfly stages
Egg: In shape typical of most lycaenids, a tiny flattened sphere; white or pale blue, pitted all over, laid singly.

Larva: Green with darker markings, pale line along edges, brown head.

Pupa: Pale, tinged greenish or pink, spotted or mottled dark brown, attached by rear end and girdle under leaf of foodplant.

Male

Adult: Male: above bluish lilac shading to brown; beneath pale grey dotted with brown and white. Female: above dull brown shading to blue; beneath same as male.

Distribution map

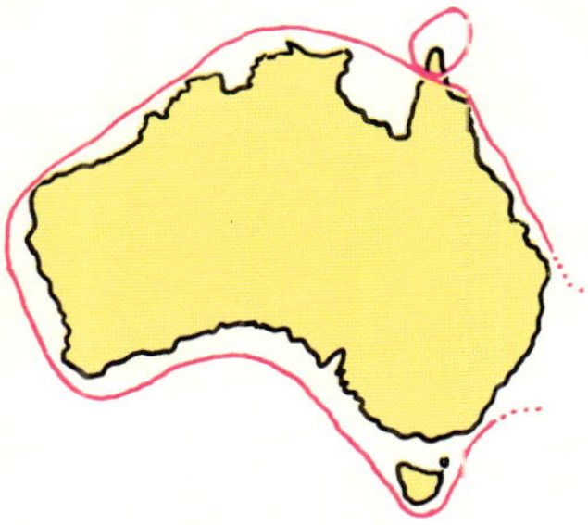

Small green-banded blue *(Danis hymetus)*

Unusually, these little butterflies are seen at their prettiest when settled with wings closed. They are usually observed only in the vicinity of the native foodplant, red ash, which is sometimes left in place in new gardens. It makes an attractive ornamental tree as well as providing food for the butterfly larvae and nectar for a number of other insects.

Larval foodplants
Native: *Alphitonia excelsa* (family Rhamnaceae), a tree known as red ash.

Butterfly stages
Egg: Small, whitish, pimply, difficult to see on underside of leaf.

Larva: Flattened, pale green with dense covering of short hairs, darker stripe and pale dorsal band. Hard to find, as it blends with the hairy underside of leaf.

Pupa: Cream with darker markings, attached under leaf.

Adult: Male: soft blue above with narrow black borders, sometimes whitish at centre; below white with wide black borders attractively patterned metallic blue-green. Female: white above with very wide black borders and some metallic blue-green; beneath same as male.

Distribution map

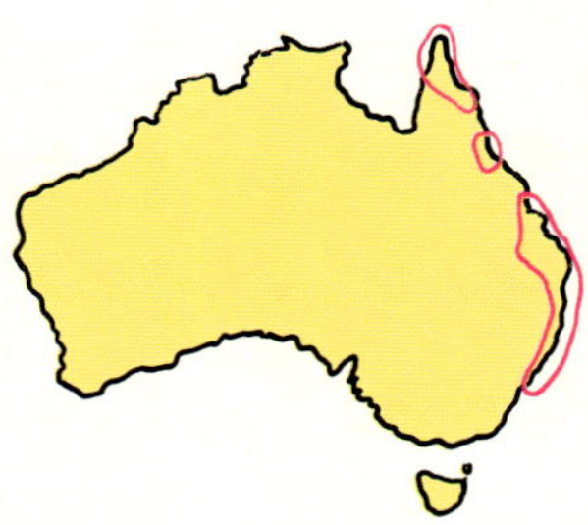

Female

Common imperial blue *(Jalmenus evagoras)*

Newly emerged male butterflies can be seen flying around the unopened pupae on their foodplants, waiting for females to emerge. There is competition among the males, and mating often takes place before a female has had time to expand her wings after emerging.

Larval foodplants
Native: Many species of *Acacia* (wattle), usually on plants under about 2 metres high. Any small acacia plant with a ragged look is worth investigating for larvae and/or pupae.

Butterfly stages
Egg: Whitish, a flattened sphere with a pattern of ridges and pimples, laid in a group, often at the junction of a branch or a depression in the stem.

Larva: Pale and speckled at first, reddish brown or green later with small tubercles, head black. When mature, dark greenish to black, a pair of fine white diagonal lines on each segment and a row of tubercles on back and along sides. Usually feeds in company, always attended by little black ants.

Pupa: Shining black, with some orange-brown markings, suspended by anal hooks and cremaster; many together along stem, also attended by ants.

Distribution map

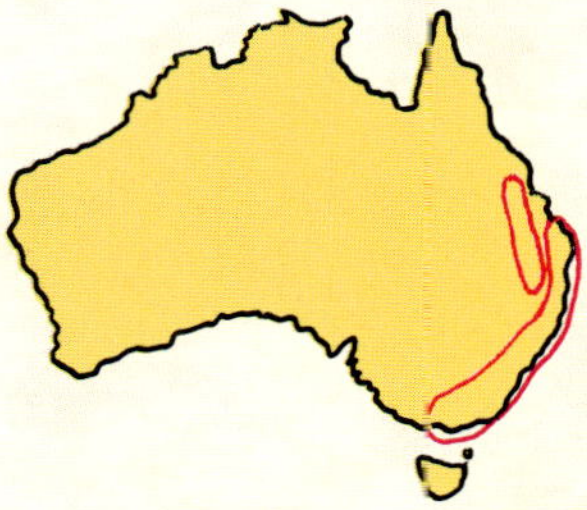

Female (left) and male (right)

Adult: Male: above metallic blue-green with very wide black borders, hindwing with two orange-red spots and fine black tail; below buff with fine black lines and bars, hindwing with red and black pattern at lower edge. Female: very similar.

Double-spotted line blue *(Nacaduba biocellata)*

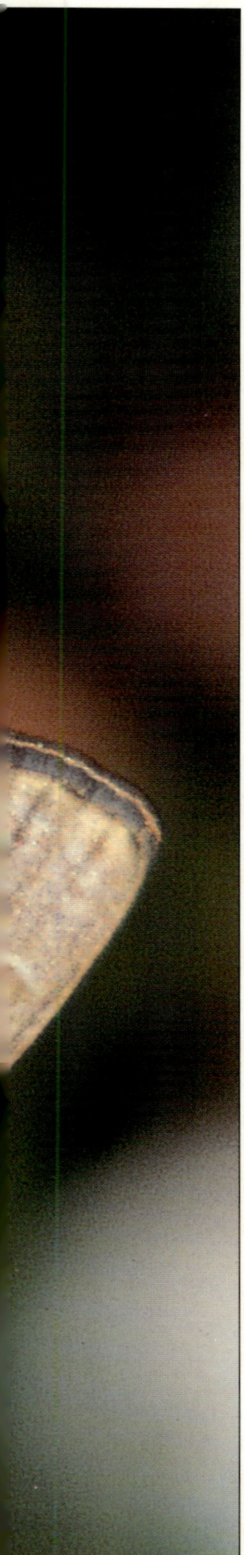

One of the smallest lycaenid butterflies, sometimes seen flying in large numbers around acacia foodplants. Larvae and pupae are attended by small black ants.

Larval foodplants
Native: Buds and flowers of several species of *Acacia* (wattle).

Butterfly stages
Egg: A flattened whitish sphere with a pitted surface, laid on flowerbuds of the foodplant.

Larva: Humped above, colour variable, often tending to match the flower – yellow, orange, green or pinkish.

Pupa: Light brown with darker spots and blotches. Found under leaf litter below foodplant, attached by anal hooks and cremaster to leaf or bark.

Adult: Male: above lilac shading to blue at base, narrow dark border, hindwing with two brown spots, no tail; beneath light yellow-brown with whitish and dark lines, hindwing with two prominent black spots edged yellowish, some metallic green scales. Female: dark brown with bluish bases, two brown spots; beneath same as male.

Female (left) and male (right)

Distribution map

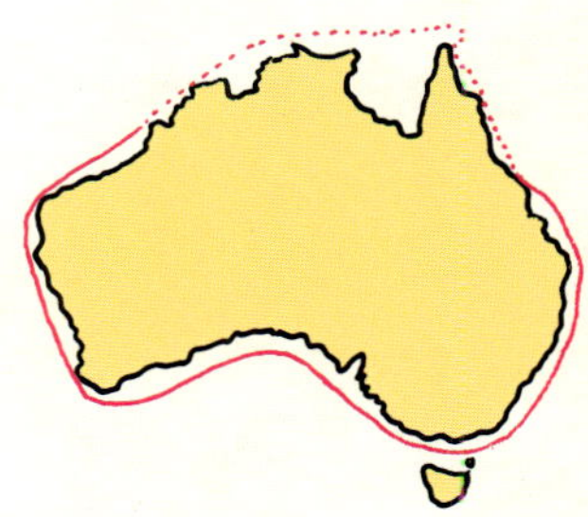

Fiery jewel *(Hypochrysops ignitus)*

Larvae and pupae are attended by small Iridomyrmex ants, and spend the day in the ants' nest or in a shelter or byre made for them by the ants.

This is a member of the most colourful group of lycaenids, well deserving the common name of 'jewel'. Together with the copper jewel, cyane jewel, peacock jewel, narcissus jewel and others, it is outstanding not only for the brilliant metallic blue, green or purple above, but for the reds and coppery patterns below – visible on a resting butterfly.

Male

Larval foodplants
Native: Many and diverse, including *Alphitonia excelsa* (red ash), *Exocarpus* (native cherry), *Dodonaea* (hop bush), *Pomaderris, Jacksonia*, several species of *Acacia* and several species of *Eucalyptus*.

Butterfly stages
Egg: A flattened white sphere covered with short spines, laid in clusters on trunk of foodplant.

Larva: Pinkish grey or brown, paler along sides; dark brown dorsal stripe constricted at front of each body segment.

Pupa: Smooth, greyish yellow but heavily marked and mottled very dark brown. Pupation in ants' nest or in shelter made by ants.

Adult: Male: above dull purple with wide dark borders, front wing with orange edge and sometimes orange suffusions; beneath light brownish, base brilliantly patterned with orange bars edged metallic blue-green, small black lines and spots. Female: above bluish purple with wide dark borders, wings more rounded than male. Beneath similar to male.

Distribution map

Male

Family Hesperiidae *(Skippers)*

Skippers, swifts and darters...these names give away one of the chief characteristics of this family of interesting but often overlooked butterflies – their swift, erratic flight. Other general features are stout bodies with short triangular wings, and broad heads with large eyes and clubbed or hooked antennae that are wide apart at the base.

While sombrely clad, most skippers are nevertheless distinctive because of their liveliness and character. They commonly fly in bright sunshine and feed freely at flowers, often remaining for some time on one bloom. While lacking the bright colours of other families, some skippers are attractively patterned. Members of one group – commonly called 'flats' – are unusual in resting and feeding with wings widespread.

The heads of hesperiid larvae are prominent, and there's the appearance of a neck as the body is usually tapered at both ends. The larvae usually feed at night and hide by day among leaves on the foodplant or in leaf litter below it. The pupae lie in shelters of leaves and silk, attached by the cremaster and sometimes supported by a silk girdle.

Skippers at rest hold their wings in one of three ways: erect like a butterfly's, flat like many moths, or with hindwings and forewings raised at an angle. Two skippers are described here, while others are pictured.

Symmomus skipper *(Trapezites symmomus)*

Easy to observe while feeding on garden flowers, this skipper holds its wings erect and together when at rest. The symmomus skipper is one of a group of closely related species whose larvae feed on the straplike leaves of Lomandra*. These native plants are common in bushland gardens, mainly because they are extraordinarily difficult to dig up! The presence of larvae in a clump of* Lomandra *is often indicated by a V-shaped notch cut out of the edge of a leaf.*

Larval foodplants
Native: *Lomandra longifolia.*

Butterfly stages
Egg: Creamy white, laid singly on or near foodplant.

Larva: Stout, pale, pinkish, brown dots all over and brown stripe above; head with deep depression or cleft above; very rough-textured; feeds at night, hides at centre of foodplant by day.

Pupa: Light brown mottled very dark, forked at front end, tip of abdomen black; found at centre of foodplant in leaves joined by silk, or nearby in dead-leaf shelter.

Male

Adult: Male and female: above dark brown to black suffused orange at base, forewing with three large yellowish patches and several smaller, hindwing with broad orange band at centre, marginal fringe chequered orange; below forewing orange-brown, dark brown at centre patterned as above, hindwing orange-brown distinctively patterned with small bluish white spots edged black and brown.

Distribution map

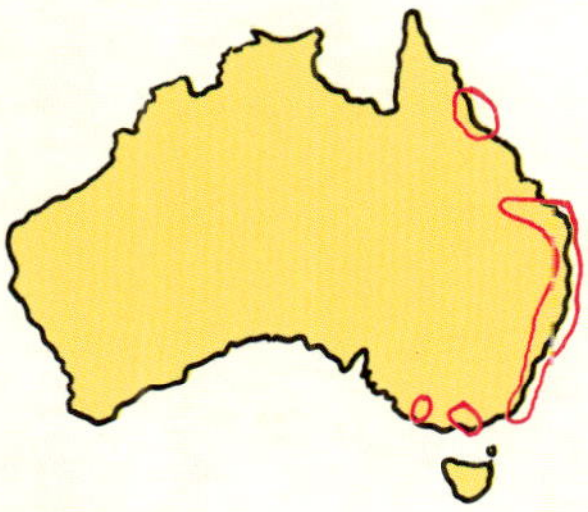

Eastern flat *(Netrocoryne repanda)*

The cutting and folding of its leaf shelter by the brightly coloured larva is reminiscent of origami and fascinating to watch. Can be raised indoors but much patience is needed as the larva is very slow to develop. The butterfly is a photographer's delight as it rests and feeds with wings spread wide, showing off the attractive semi-transparent wing-spots.

Larval foodplants
Exotic: Camphor laurel (*Cinnamomum camphora*).

Native: Mainly *Callicoma serratifolia* but also corkwood (*Endiandra sieberi*), brush box (*Lophostemon confertus*), lilly-pilly (*Acmena smithii*), *Elaeocarpus* and kurrajong (*Brachychiton populneum*).

Larva: At first yellowish and hairy. On hatching it constructs a daytime shelter nearby, cutting an almost complete circle out of the leaf, bending it over and fixing it down with silk. When older the brightly patterned yellow, black and bluish grey larva makes a silk-lined shelter out of the leaf by cutting, folding and 'stitching' it, then chewing partway through midrib so end section dies. Feeds at night on original and adjacent leaves.

Pupa: Stout with short hairs, head with forked projection, dark grey in front with bluish waxy powder; abdomen whitish with large black spot near front partly covered by wings; pupates in larval shelter.

Female

Adult: Male: above dark brown, forewing with translucent whitish patches and spots edged dark brown, hindwing with single translucent spot; beneath shaded light to dark brown, similar patches and spots. Female: similar, spots larger, hindwing with yellowish streak.

Distribution map

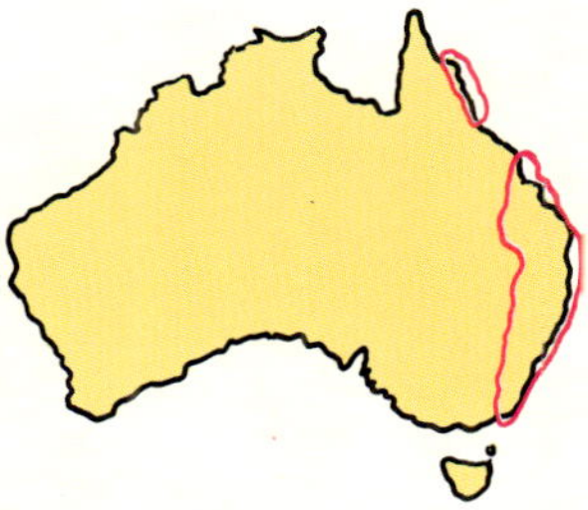

Butterfly Foodplants

Exotic

Artemisia spp.	Australian painted lady
Bean, broad	Common grass blue
Bean, garden	Common grass blue
Bird-of-paradise shrub (*Caesalpinia gilliesii*)	Tailed emperor
Brazilian ironwood (*Caesalpinia ferrea*)	Tailed emperor
Broccoli	Cabbage white
Buffalo grass	Evening brown
Cabbage	Cabbage white
Camphor laurel (*Cinnamomum camphora*)	Macleay's swallowtail
	Blue triangle
	Eastern flat skipper
Candlestick cassia (*Cassia alata*)	Tailed emperor
Capeweed	Australian painted lady
Cassia nodosa	Lemon migrant
Cauliflower	Cabbage white
Chilean jasmine (*Mandevillea*)	Common Australian crow
Citrus (cultivated orange, lemon, etc.)	Orchard swallowtail
	Dingy swallowtail
	Chequered swallowtail
	Ulysses (possibly)
Clover	Common grass blue
Cottonbush (*Asclepias* spp.)	Wanderer
Crepe myrtle (*Lagerstroemia indica*)	Tailed emperor
Cudweed	Australian painted lady
Elm (*Ulmus* spp.)	Tailed emperor
False acacia (*Robinia pseudoacacia*)	Tailed emperor
Ganges bluebell (*Asystasia gangetica*)	Common eggfly
Golden-rain tree (*Cassia fistula*)	Tailed emperor
	Lemon migrant
Grass, couch	Common brown ringlet
Grasses, various	Common brown
	Common brown ringlet
	Evening brown
Lavender	Australian painted lady (reported)
Lucerne	Common grass blue
Mignonette	Cabbage white
Milkweeds (*Asclepias* spp.)	Wanderer
Millet	Evening brown
Moth plant (*Araujia hortorum*)	Wanderer
Mustard	Cabbage white
Nasturtium (*Tropaeolum majus*)	Cabbage white
Oleander (*Nerium* sp.)	Common Australian crow
Paspalum	Evening brown
Pea, garden	Common grass blue

Pink-and-white shower	Lemon migrant
Plantain	Meadow argus
Poinciana (*Delonix regia*)	Tailed emperor
Polygonum prostratum	Common eggfly
Portulaca	Meadow argus
	Common eggfly
Psoralea pinnata	Chequered swallowtail
Purple top, snakebush (*Verbena bonariensis*)	Meadow argus
Scotch thistle	Australian painted lady
Snapdragon	Meadow argus
Spider flower (*Cleome* sp.)	Cabbage white
Star jasmine (*Trachelospermum* sp.)	Common Australian crow
Stephanotis sp.	Common Australian crow
Stinging nettle (*Urtica urens*)	Australian admiral
Sugarcane	Evening brown
Turnip	Cabbage white
Verbena spp.	Meadow argus

Native

Note: where a species has a wide range of foodplants, a selection only is given.

Acacia spp.	Tailed emperor
	Common grass yellow
	Common imperial blue
	Fiery jewel
Acmena smithii	Eastern flat
Albizia lophantha	Tailed emperor
Alphitonia excelsa	Small green-banded blue
	Fiery jewel
Alternanthera denticulata	Common eggfly
Apopyllum anomalum	Caper white
Aristolochia spp.	Birdwing
Blueberry ash (*Alphitonia* sp.)	Eastern flat
Brachychiton populneum	Tailed emperor
	Eastern flat
Breynia spp.	Common grass yellow
Brush box	Eastern flat
Callicoma serratifolia	Eastern flat
Caper	Caper white
Capparis spp.	Caper white
Cassia spp.	Common grass yellow
	Lemon migrant
Corkwood	Eastern flat
Crested wattle	Tailed emperor
Daisy family (some)	Australian painted lady
Desmodium sp.	Common grass blue
Dodonaea spp.	Fiery jewel
Drypetes australasica	Common albatross

Elaeocarpus spp.	Eastern flat
Endiandra sieberi	Eastern flat
Eremocitrus spp.	Dingy swallowtail
Eriostemon spp.	Orchard butterfly
Eucalyptus spp.	Fiery jewel
Euodia bonwickii	Ulysses
Euodia elleryana	Ulysses
Exocarpus spp.	Fiery jewel
Ficus spp.	Common Australian crow
Fig	Common Australian crow
Gahnia spp.	Swordgrass brown
Glycine sp.	Common grass blue
Goodenia spp.	Meadow argus
Hop bush	Fiery jewel
Hoya australis	Common Australian crow
Imperata sp.	Common brown ringlet
Indigofera sp.	Common grass blue
Jacksonia spp.	Fiery jewel
Joyweed	Common eggfly
Kangaroo grass	Common brown
Kurrajong	Tailed emperor Eastern flat
Leichhardtia australis	Common Australian crow
Lomandra longifolia	Symmomus skipper
Lotus sp.	Common grass blue
Microcitrus spp.	Dingy swallowtail
Mistletoes, various	Common jezabel Wood white
Native cherry	Fiery jewel
Paddy's lucerne	Common eggfly
Pomaderris sp.	Fiery jewel
Psoralia spp.	Chequered swallowtail Common grass blue
Red ash	Small green-banded blue Fiery jewel
Scaevola spp.	Meadow argus
Sida rhombifolia	Common eggfly
Stinging nettle	Australian admiral
Swordgrass	Swordgrass brown
Themeda australis	Common brown
Tristania conferta	Eastern flat
Urtica incisa	Australian admiral
Wattle spp.	Tailed emperor